Limpet Stew and Potato Jelly

Occupation Recipes

Christopher Addy

We're all quite well, but getting thinner
Not much for tea, still less for dinner
Though not exactly on our uppers
We've said 'Adieu' to cold ham suppers

Jersey
Heritage

First published Jersey 2014

by Jersey Heritage
Text copyright © Jersey Heritage Trust
Illustrations courtesy of Jersey Heritage/Société Jersiaise
Collection unless otherwise credited.

Front cover: Queuing for vegetables in Halkett Place. Courtesy
of Jersey War Tunnels Collection.

ISBN 978-0-9562079-5-1

Contents

Foreword

In 1994 when the Jersey Museums Service published Lillie Aubin Morris' collection of Occupation Recipes it was simply that, a collection of recipes. When it was suggested that we revisit the subject, I decided that the recipes should be set in their historical context. In this short volume Occupation historian Christopher Addy writes about the difficulties faced by Islanders during the five years the island was held by the Germans, the importance of the International Red Cross vessels - especially the *Vega* - in staving off mass starvation, the ingenuity of islanders in finding substitute foods and the impact of five years of controlled diet on islanders' health.

The illustration are taken from the Jersey Heritage/Société Jersiaise, the Damien Horn and the Jersey War Tunnels collections.

The concluding chapter carries the recipes. For ease of reading, they have been divided into sections - otherwise they are as written. The compilation gives the reader a fascinating insight into the everyday life of Islanders during that period. While it is still possible to find the ingredients and cook them I would imagine the taste may seem a little lacking to the modern palate.

Doug Ford
Jersey Heritage
January 2014

Chapter 1:
The context of hunger

Whilst the rationing of meats, butter and sugar was introduced in the Channel Islands at the time of the outbreak of hostilities, as it was in the United Kingdom, the arrival of the German occupying forces on 1 June 1940 created a whole new scenario - placing enduring strains on the supply of food and other consumables to the local population.

German soldiers outside 'Edwards Charing Cross Bazaar' in King Street, St Helier.

The most obvious was the cessation of imports, upon which the 41,101 civilian inhabitants were heavily reliant, and then there was, as Sonia Hillsdon described in her book *Jersey Occupation Remembered*, the first influx of 'great swarms of soldiers in the shops buying up as fast as they could.' Their purchasing, particularly of luxury goods, was so rampant that it was soon curtailed by order at the end of the first week of July 1940. The response by those islanders who could afford it was panic-buying on the understanding that there would be no replenishment of stocks and this led to the additional rationing of salt, tea, coffee, cocoa and cooking fat on a weekly basis. After the first year of Occupation the strength of the military force stabilised at around 11,000 men.

Rationing, which was to fluctuate widely during the five years of Occupation, was further extended in the Islands in September 1940 to impose more strict controls upon the distribution of meat, sugar, tea, butter, milk and cooking fats. Seasonal fruit and vegetables grown on the Island, such as potatoes, tomatoes, carrots, swedes and parsnips, were not rationed. Each adult was given a ration book with the coupons inside being exchanged for goods. The average person's weekly adult ration in May 1941 was:

11 ozs meat	927 calories (later there were often meatless days)
2 ozs. butter	438
2 ozs cooking fat	527
3 ozs sugar	349
4 ozs wheat flour	415
4 ozs oatmeal	472
3.3 pints milk	1,323 (1 pint per day for children)
Total weekly	**10,835**
Total daily	**1,548 calories**

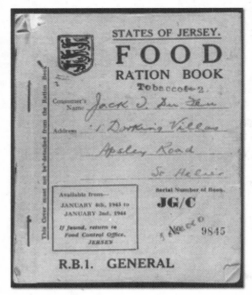

Ration book.

These rations, although imbalanced and deficient in fats and protein were sufficient to sustain life. They did require supplementary vegetables to meet the minimum daily calorific requirement.

Shortly after the outset of the Occupation, the Channel Islands Purchasing Commission was established with a view to sourcing food and other supplies in France. With headquarters in Granville the agents from Jersey and Guernsey travelled far and wide to establish trade contacts and seek out food and other essential items. However, it wasn't until 1941 that their efforts began to reap real rewards, and prove to be a crucial means of substantiating local resources. Some of the food items that were regularly imported were potatoes, flour, salt, and macaroni, whilst medicines, clothing and agricultural equipment were also supplied. With bread rationing commencing in August 1941, seed wheat was also imported and sown, necessitating the use of redundant threshing machines and the reopening of the island's water mills for its grinding.

After 1942 the Purchasing Committee was unable to source pork and poultry, nor did they import any fish. Despite being surrounded by the sea, islanders were unable to exploit this food resource due to the German fear of escapees furnishing the Allies with important military information. Sea fishing could only be undertaken within fixed hours and with an escort and permit - however, these were only issued to married fishermen without English relations, as spouses served as insurance of their return. Fishermen were also required to paint their boats with bands of blue, white and red, and give 20 percent of their catches to the Germans on their return.

Access to shore gathering was severely restricted as much of the island's coastline was heavily mined) and declared off limits to civilians. Where low-water and rod

fishing were allowed the seashore was foraged for limpets, razor fish, ormers, sand eels and winkles, which also served to feed domestic animals. The Germans themselves requisitioned tennis nets which, pegged out in large C-shapes in St Brelade's Bay, were effective fish traps.

Tobacco, clothing and footwear were also controlled and, over the course of time, the prices of these commodities were to increase so dramatically that they were simply unaffordable. The nature of goods that could be sold at auction was also controlled, prohibiting the unscrupulous from 'cashing in'. Despite these attempts at control, goods regarded as luxuries commanded extraordinary prices. In 1945 tea was fetching £20-£30 per pound and a pound of tobacco went for £112.

During the course of the Occupation, many would be convicted for engaging in the illicit black market. The entry in Leslie Sinel's *Occupation Diary* for 31 December 1941 stated:

> *'The black market is flourishing and there has been an enormous amount of meat changing hands of late; poultry is very plentiful and is fetching absurd prices, some turkeys being sold in the region of £15 to £20.'*

Common food-related criminal charges were the breaching of price controls, the illegal sale of controlled foods and the failure of farmers to supply the requisite milk quantities to the German forces. Of course those who lived in the country benefitted from a greater access to meat and dairy products, often as the result of the outwitting of German food inspectors. The theft of foodstuffs was to reach epidemic proportions.

Residents of St Helier without country relatives struggled to manage on rations alone; these were enhanced by the occasional surprise of a special ration of nuts,

St Brelade's Bay, requisitioned tennis nets put in a large U shape to act as fish traps.

butter or cheese, and by reliance upon their wits. The importance of the States of Jersey communal kitchen in Phillips Street, managed by Miss Fraser, the St Helier House Community Restaurant at Chelsea House (later taken over by the Sun Works) and the various soup kitchens, cannot be over-estimated.

Whilst the black market was, for those who could afford it, a useful means of substantiating the meagre ration, there was a general shift towards payments being settled in the form of produce, and the prevalence of bartering and exchange. The Evening Post classifieds advertised many such opportunities under 'Exchange and Mart' on a daily basis. Shirley Barr remembers:

'Father, because there was no replenishment of stock, used to barter for things. The Germans came in and so he would get what he could out of them and would let them have that for a loaf of bread. I think that was really how a lot of people did it. A lot of people were honest enough not to take advantage, to try and make a reasonable deal, but then you see, Dad did buy meat off the black market to keep us alive. We were at the stage where we were growing rapidly, Marion and I, because we were young teenagers. It was a very difficult age to bring up children…Mother was very, very thin, and had been quite ill during the war.'

The Soup Queue at Biberach.

The castle at Wurzach, Germany.

In September 1942 the first of 2,200 Channel Islanders were deported to internment camps, most of which were located in Southern Germany. These deportations were ordered by Hitler in retaliation for the British internment of German nationals in Iran in 1941. Jersey families ended up in Wurzach, where they were accommodated in an 18th century castle; food shortages

Group portrait of Organisation Todt workers at l'Etacq, mostly Ukrainians. the man at far right is a Russian student interpreter. Reclining at the front, 3rd from the right is Francisco Font, later a Jersey resident.

The Gloucester Street Prison, St Helier.

were initially extreme, before a regular supply of Red Cross food parcels began in December 1942. Additionally, soup was issued twice a day; its varieties were given exotic names by the internees, amusingly at odds with their flavour and content. Red cabbage soup was known as 'Blue Danube' due to its colour, and millet soup 'Black Forest' because of the bits of twig floating in it.

In the Island general shortages were further exacerbated when thousands of forced and slave workers were brought to the island to work on the fortifications under the Organisation Todt between late 1941 and mid 1943. Whilst their rations came in from the Continent, corruption at the harbour, in conjunction with the totally inadequate quantities, made it necessary for them to risk leaving their camps to forage, beg and steal food and clothing, and seek shelter from the local people. Their arrival also brought an increase in skin conditions and aided the spread of diphtheria in the 1943 epidemic. Sadly several Algerian forced workers, in their hungry desperation, ate hemlock and suffered an agonising death.

For those unlucky enough to find themselves incarcerated in Jersey's prison in late 1944, as a consequence of 'political' offences against the Occupying Forces, meals consisted of subsistence quantities of ersatz coffee, dry bread, swedes, watery 'soup', potatoes and 'porridge'. Prisoners were largely reliant upon family members to bring in food and other essentials.

Chapter 2:
Salvation in the form of the
International Red Cross

The long-awaited Allied Invasion in June 1944 inspired islanders to seriously consider the imminence of liberation; when one could witness the progress of the American 6th Army from the east coast, it was reasonable to assume that it was only a matter of days, or weeks at the most, before the islands were to be freed. However, as those weeks passed, anticipation turned to resentment and then to resignation that the Allies weren't coming.

By late July German rations were down to three months supply, then in early August, with the fall of Granville and St Malo, all supplies ceased. Hitler was informed and agreed that Britain be approached to discuss the evacuation of all civilians not working on the land, or the sending of emergency food relief. Hence, on 19 September the German Foreign Ministry asked the Protecting Power, Switzerland, to inform Britain that supplies for the civilian population were exhausted, proposing

International Red Cross ship SS Vega moored in St Helier Harbour.

those alternatives; Churchill supported the evacuation of women and children, but was entirely against sending food in, anticipating it being purloined by the Germans.

What resulted was a lengthy debate concerning whose responsibility it was to feed the civilians. However on 7 November Churchill agreed to allow the

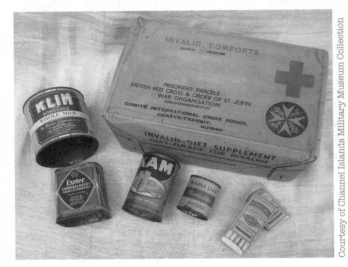

Red Cross parcel.

importation of food parcels and medical supplies as long as the Germans continued to be responsible for the civilian population. The SS *Vega* of the International Red Cross arrived in St Peter Port harbour on 27 December 1944, sailing to Jersey on New Year's Eve; every civilian was to receive two Red Cross parcels, each weighing 9 lbs 10ozs. They contained:

6 ozs chocolate
20 biscuits
4 ozs tea
20 ozs butter
6 ozs sugar
2 ozs milk powder
1lb tin marmalade
5 oz tin sardines
8 oz packet of raisins
6 oz packet prunes
4 oz packet of cheese
3 oz tablet of soap
1 oz each of pepper and salt

Kettle fashioned from a food tin.

As demonstrated by Channel Island internees who had been deported to internment camps on the Continent, it wasn't just the contents of the containers which were useful. Once the food was consumed, the tins could be fashioned into cooking or drinking vessels, flattened and joined to make baking dishes, or used imaginatively for crafts.

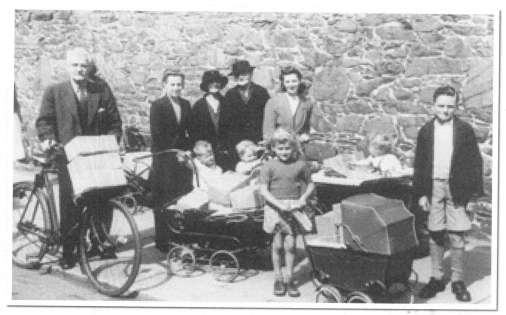

Families walking along Gloucester Street, St Helier after collecting their Red Cross Parcels.

Whilst the occupiers honoured their word that they would not interfere with the Red Cross parcels, they soon increased the volume of goods requisitioned from civilian stocks, despite careful attempts by members of the States of Jersey Superior Council to manipulate stock figures to the benefit of the population. Searches for illicit private hoards were instituted, with one islander surrendering 186 tins of soup, vegetables and fish and 286 bottles of alcoholic drinks. Soon it became clear that the civilians had more to eat than the Germans; Leslie Sinel's entry in his *Occupation Diary* for 28 February 1945 reads:

> 'They are very hungry and will do almost anything to obtain food, some having even been seen rummaging in dustbins...Numbers of dogs and cats are missing, these now figuring on German menus. The Germans have also proper squads of limpet-pickers, their "catch" helping - with sugar beet - to flavour "soup"!'

The SS *Vega* visited the Islands a total of six times, delivering over 100,000 food parcels and 4,200 invalid diet parcels, and undoubtedly saving the Islanders from the horrors of starvation.

Chapter 3:
Substitute or Ersatz foods - making the best of what one had

Against this background of scarcity, parents struggled to put adequate meals on the table for their families. The abiding characteristic of food preparation, and indeed daily life in general, was the importance of taking an imaginative and pragmatic attitude towards substitution.

As it was necessary to harness the nutritional value of locally grown produce, sometimes domestic implements had to be designed from scratch for the purpose. Despite the best efforts of foragers to glean sheaves of corn or oats left behind by the farmer, wheat flour was generally unavailable. Instead some islanders turned to the humble potato in order to facilitate baking; Alan Nicolle describes below the method widely used which, on average, would produce one pound of 'flour' from ten pounds of potatoes.

Potato Grater.
Courtesy of Jersey War Tunnels Collection

'My father had a wooden mincing machine made out of wood and the business part inside was this old bean tin, which he'd punched holes through from the inside; quite a lot of holes in fact. I think it must have had a wooden plate on one end, or both ends, because it had to be pivoted, and a wooden handle. Very much an old fashioned mincing machine and the potatoes used to be pushed in the top and grated. The pulp was then put into a bath of water, an old oval-shaped galvanised bath, and was left to stand overnight. Then the pulp was very carefully taken out and squeezed and the result was a sort of milky looking fluid left in this bath. It was left to settle until it cleared then you could see this white deposit on the bottom about an inch or 25mm thick. And very carefully the water would be scooped off so as not to disturb the sediment. And then eventually when you got it down until there was just a little drop of water on the top, it was very carefully drained off and then this white deposit was scraped out, put on newspaper and spread out in the sun and dried. You had to be very careful that it didn't blow away in the wind. It was quite a lengthy job but it could be used as a form of flour. It was old potatoes that were used, not very good ones.'

Sugar Beet Press.
Courtesy of Jersey War Tunnels Collection

In fact, as Margaret Bird recalled in 1974, 'flour' became a generic term that could be in actuality oatmeal, barley flour, or bean flour, whilst 'sugar' was normally sugar beet syrup, another ingredient which required the manufacture of dedicated apparatus - the sugar beet press. The process was just as laborious as the aforementioned - often 20lbs of beet would harvest 4lbs of syrup.

'To make sugar beet syrup, one bought a hundredweight of sugar beet and scrubbed them clean, sliced them and cooked them in the copper in the wash-house. I was lucky that I had some friends who did some tree felling and they were able to let me have faggots of twigs, which were...useful to me to get the copper going. Having got the beet soft, it then had to be squeezed so that all the juice came out of it - an extremely difficult job that was - and then one had to reduce all this juice by boiling it and boiling it. So after several days of hard work - and it was hard work - one finished up with about 6 or 7 jam jars full of dark treacly stuff which one spread on a bit of hard bake (bread), and I can assure you that that was very satisfying indeed.'

Beyond the food itself, there was also a terrible deficit of fuel for cooking. Whilst some turned to burning cabbage stumps, bakehouses offered a community service; when bread baking was complete, islanders would arrive with their sugar beet for dry-roasting or earthenware casseroles, stone jam jars or baking tins full with *'all kinds of concoctions - some smelling much better than others when cooked!'* Visits to the bakehouse also presented an opportunity to exchange news.

Fuel rationing began in the Island in October 1941, when only wood was available; there was thenceforth a steady decline in the issue of domestic fuel, with gas running out completely in September 1944, and electricity early the following year. With the eventual restriction of bakehouse cooking, ingenuity was again the order of the day; Shirley Barr recalls:

'You could cook the food up to a certain point and then pop it in the hay box which cooked it. Dad managed to get some wheat and...grind that down to make wheat porridge. You got it up to boiling point, pop it in the hay box and leave it over night and then in the morning it was lovely porridge. It was basically a slow cooker. He made it up in a box; mother put a couple of pans in and he stuffed it all round these pans, the hay was packed right down so mother had two sorts of nests to put the saucepans in. Dad had packed it really solidly, and then an old

piece of eiderdown in the lid and then a lid on top of that. It was quite a big thing.'

Hay box stoves were also fabricated by Channel Island deportees at Biberach internment camp, to help keep drinks warm. Another ingenious device was the sawdust stove; essentially a cylinder with a vent at its base and trivet on the top, the sawdust would burn slowly over a long period, providing minimal heat for the pan above.

In relation to supplies of meat, the meticulous documentation of livestock made it difficult to slaughter illegally, tricking the Germans out of their strict quotas, but it did occur regularly, feeding an illicit meat

Courtesy of Jersey War Tunnels Collection

Queuing for vegetables in Halkett Place.

Queuing at Tanguy's Dairy.

trade with rapidly escalating prices. Most Islanders have heard stories of the pig in bed with grandma, who was too ill to get up for the German house search! Meanwhile, the once abundant wild rabbit became an increasingly attractive target for those with the agility and skill to use string nets to catch them. Whilst vegetables were not rationed, when an allocation was available, hours of tedious queuing were required in order to take home trifling amounts. Some of these vegetables lent themselves to diverse purposes, as Marjorie Bird writes:

'After the last tea ration in February 1941 we made a substitute from grated and dried carrots. We also made parsnips into 'coffee' and 'grape-nuts' cereals from sugar beet. Dried bramble leaves could be used as 'tea' or even smoked.'

Joe Mière, whose family lived in Midvale Road, St Helier, has reminisced that his family roasted acorns and used a traditional hand-grinder to create a 'coffee' powder; barley was also a common coffee substitute. Others collected Carrageen

German soldiers collecting seawater.

Moss, known also as Irish Moss; this frilly seaweed has gelatinous qualities which when boiled and added to milk, would produce a nutritious blancmange, whilst others used it to make hair cream.

In addition buckets of seawater could be evaporated down to form precious salt crystals, enhancing the otherwise bland and repetitive flavours of the staple diet; the Germans were also reduced to this in the final period of the Occupation. Chemists also played an important role in synthesising flavourings and sweeteners which no doubt added interest to an otherwise begrudging intake.

Chapter 4:
The effects of the Occupation diet upon the health of the population

The effects of food shortages on the health of the islanders were varied but not all bad. Cases of diarrhoea or colitis, otherwise known as the *'Jersey Rattles'*, were widespread as a consequence of the roughage-rich vegetarian diet. When bread was being made on the Island, cases of constipation rose sharply. However, the reduction in alcohol, tobacco, fat and sugar had a positive influence on the medical and dental health of the population, who also benefitted from the all-encompassing requisition of motor vehicles, ensuring an increase in the exercise rates of the overweight.

Despite there being no general increase in the death rate during the Occupation, by 1941 deaths from tuberculosis (TB) were 50% above the UK national average. The Island's Medical Board, formed in December 1940, allocated additional rations for distribution to pregnant women and those suffering from diabetes or TB. Poor nutrition, due to a lack of vitamins in the diet, left islanders lacking in energy and with weakened powers of concentration. Islanders also became more susceptible to skin infections such as lice, ringworm, impetigo and scabies, due to the lack of soap. Known generically as 'Occupation dermatitis', the treatment was to scrub the skin with tar ointment, which looked and smelled awful. The deficit in foodstuffs also affected the recovery time from injury; small cuts often became infected, sometimes developing into more serious ulcers.

There was a severe shortage of drugs and medical equipment throughout the period; Dr Noel McKinstry, the Medical Officer of Health, developed vaccines, vitamins and lotions from the materials at hand. Once cod liver oil ran out, he improvised by steaming fish livers; when the thyroid supply dried up, he obtained thyroid glands from animals at the abattoir. By late 1943 cotton wool had run out, and compressed paper was used instead; bandages were washed and reused and there were calls to the public for mosquito netting and ballet dress fabric for use as substitute dressings.

The post-war findings of Dr McKinstry as to the cumulative effect of the Occupation upon the general health of the islanders were that malnutrition affected a reduction in children's height of approximately half an inch (1¼ cms), and that the average weight for children was 4lbs (1¾ kgs) below normal. Whilst there was a slight increase in the death rate, factors other than food, such as inadequate heating and clothing, fear and depression were also seen to be significant contributory factors.

Recipes

But what of the application of these ingredients and the exotic recipes in which they featured. Fortunately Lillie Aubin Morris, who lived at Pontac, St Clement with her husband and twin sons, recorded this collection of Occupation recipes for posterity. Some were hand written, whilst others were taken from the Evening Post which regularly published advice from Miss J Fraser, the States cookery expert, as well as suggestions from readers.

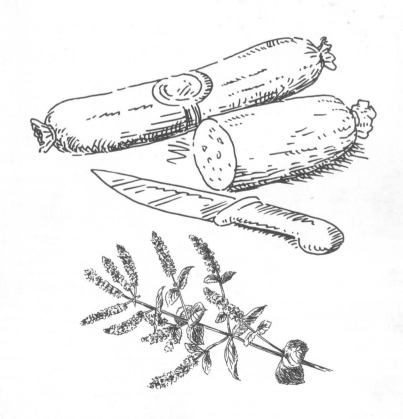

Chapter 5:
A Collection of Occupation Recipes by Lillie Aubin Morris

Breakfast

With private cars all requisitioned people had to walk or cycle to work and school. They needed something solid to start their day.

Breakfast scones

1 lb flour
2 teaspoonful baking powder
or egg powder
Small teaspoonful salt
About a breakfast cupful of milk

Mix all the ingredients together, then gradually add the milk till you have a moderately soft dough. Knead a little, then roll out on a floured board till about half an inch thick. Cut into three-cornered pieces and bake at once in a hot oven.

These scones can be buttered or served with jam.

To make sweet scones:

Add 2ozs currents or sultanas and 1oz sugar. Would be improved by the addition of 1 or 2ozs fat but quite good without.

Miss M Le Bas

Savoury Breakfast Rissoles

About 1 lb previously cooked vegetables, at least half of which should be potatoes
Parsley or mixed herbs
Breakfast cupful of bread crumbs
Salt and pepper

Well mash vegetables, add a good sprinkling of chopped parsley or herbs, add bread crumbs. Place a little flour or oatmeal flour on a saucer. Place a tablespoonful of this mixture on to the saucer and shape into small flat rissoles, turning them in flour to prevent them becoming sticky. Fry in dripping or if none available, bake in a hot oven. Then warm up again in the morning.

Mrs Le Quesne

Beverages

Porridge Rissoles

Make a thick porridge with a half cupful of oatmeal flour to 1 cup of water, cook for 10 minutes. Then stir in 2 cupful of mashed potatoes. Leave till cold, then turn into rissoles and fry or bake. Season well.

Gruel or infants' food

1 teaspoonful barley flour
½ pint milk
Sugar

Mix the flour very smoothly with a little cold milk. Heat the remainder of the milk. When boiling pour over the mixed barley flour, stirring well. Turn into a rinsed pan and place over heat. Bring to the boil stirring all the time. Cook for five to seven minutes and sweeten to taste.

Cocoa substitute drink

1 ½ teaspoonsful cocoa substitute
1 breakfast cupful water or milk and water
sugar to taste

Mix cocoa with a little milk or water till smooth. Pour on the remainder of the liquid and turn into a small pan. Bring to the boil and cook for about five minutes. Strain to keep back sediment.

NB The sediment can be kept and used for flavouring and for colouring puddings.

Tomato juice

Here is a simple way of preserving tomato juice together with its valuable vitamin C for winter use.

Wipe the tomatoes, cut in four and put in a pan (without water), and bring slowly to the boil. Boil hard for 15 minutes, strain to remove all skin and pips. Warm bottles (with small necks). Boil the juice hard for another 10 minutes. Pour into bottles, cover bottles with paper jam-pot covers, securing with rubber bands, or corks, then cool very slowly by standing the bottles in a basket or box with a pillow at the bottom and a rug or blanket wrapped around the bottles.

This juice will make delicious tomato soup, a nourishing drink or sauce throughout the winter.

Soups

Five minute tomato soup

1 Oxo cube
1 small peeled onion
Tomato purée
½ pint boiling water
1 teaspoon butter
Salt and pepper to taste

Melt butter in a saucepan, add chopped onion, simmer till soft. Dissolve Oxo in water, add an onion and butter. Flavour to taste with tomato purée or ketchup if you haven't any purée. Salt and pepper to taste. Serve with toast.

Scotch Tomato Soup

2 Oxo cubes
1 tablespoon minced parsley
2 tablespoons minced onion
1 tin tomato soup
1 quart boiling water
Salt and pepper to taste

Dissolve Oxo in water, add remainder of ingredients. Stir till boiling. Serve with thin toast.

Brown Vegetable Soup

2 quarts water
1 slice of bread
1 cabbage
2 carrots
1 turnip
2 onions or leeks
2 or 3 potatoes
Parsley, salt and pepper
1 tablespoon of oil or 1 oz butter

Fry a sliced onion or leek in the oil or butter in a large saucepan. When it is brown but not burnt, add 2 quarts of water, salt, pepper, a slice of stale bread toasted, vegetables cut up into small pieces, and a bunch of parsley. It makes a very good soup. French beans, green peas (in tins), parsnips or any other vegetable may be added. Boil for three or four hours, then mash the vegetables through a colander or in a saucepan with a spoon. Boil for another ten minutes and the soup is ready. If too thick add more water and boil for ten minutes after putting in the water. If too thin boil fast with lid off the pan until it is thick enough.

Fish

Many people, working in all sorts of jobs, obtained fishermen's permits so that they were allowed onto the shore to gather limpets and razor fish.

Limpet Stew or Curry

1 quart limpets
1 pint green peas
Thyme, parsley, one small bayleaf
1 tablespoon flour
Salt and pepper

Put the limpets in to boiling water; boil for 10 minutes. Remove shells and intestines. Then take the soft top off and mince the hard part. Put a little fat, butter or oil in frying pan. When hot add flour, a little salt, bayleaf, thyme and parsley. Fry till brown, stirring all the time. Add enough stock or water to make a thick gravy, add limpets and peas (strained), stir and simmer for 15 minutes. Excellent with two tablespoonsful of curry powder. Serve in a well of mashed potatoes or rice.

Fishcakes "Aux Pauvres"

1 pint cooked limpets
1 lb potatoes
1 medium sized onion or shallots
Salt, pepper, parsley

Remove horns and black part from limpets. Then pass whole through mincing machine. Roll small portions in flour and a fry in a little fat, or grease a baking tin and bake in a moderate oven for about one hour.

Limpet Omelette

2 quarts limpets
Bayleaf, 2 small leeks, parsley
1 egg
Pepper and salt

Put limpets in cold water, bring to the boil, then strain and remove shells. Simmer with a little pepper and salt, and bayleaf, until quite tender. Then strain, remove head and string, mince the limpets and add the leeks chopped finely. Mix together with parsley. Put a little fat into a frying-pan. Put an egg well beaten into the pan and add the limpets. Fry until brown. A very savoury dish.

Razor fish

Many people find that these fish are tough when cooked, but if cooked in the following way they are tender, nourishing and satisfying.

Place the fish in water to spit out the sand. Leave for a time, Wash in several waters until free of sand and dirt. Then place in a basin and pour boiling water over, when the shells will open. Take the fish out of the shells and pinch each one to pinch out any sand left in. Then open the fish to make sure no sand is left inside. Put them in a dish and just cover with the water they have been opened in, but strain it. Let them stand until cold. Drain and pass through a mincer, finishing off with a slice of bread to soak up any liquor. Put the minced fish into a saucepan and just cover with the liquor they have stood in. Simmer for ten minutes then thicken up with flour mixed with milk, season with pepper and salt, and serve on toast or with mashed potatoes.

Fish pudding

Tin pilchards
Parsley
1 egg
1 pt milk
6 tablespoonsful flour
1 pinch salt

Make a batter, then grease a tin, place fish in bottom, mix parsley into batter and pour over fish. Bake for 1½ hours.

Your Tunny Fish Ration

How to make the most of it!

Miss Fraser, States' domestic and cookery expert, has kindly sent us the following details as to how the best use may be made of this week's ration of tunny fish:-

Tunny fish is a fish resembling the mackerel. It is caught in the Mediterranean and also in the North Sea off Scarborough. It is preserved in oil and exported. The flesh is delicate in flavour and highly esteemed, being somewhat like veal.

Tunny fish cakes

Tin of tunny fish
4-6 tablespoons mashed potato
1 teaspoon chopped parsley
Pepper and salt

Flake the fish and mix with the oil from the tin used for preserving. Mash the potatoes, fish, seasoning and parsley together. Divide into equal portions (4-6) make each portion into a round flat cake. Brush over with milk and dredge with flour, pressing flour well on to each cake. Place on a lightly greased tin and put in oven to become lightly browned. NB chopped chives or powdered herbs can be used in place of parsley. More or less potato can be used. If wished, and the supply of fat permits, the fish cakes could be fried.

Tunny fish pie

Proportion of fish and potatoes as above, but instead of making into cakes put the mixture into a lightly greased pie dish or pyrex dish and bake.

Tunny fish paste

Mix the fish very well with the oil. Pound thoroughly and if time permits rub through a sieve. Season very well, adding a little vinegar if possible. Put the mixture into a small jar, cover down tightly and use as a sandwich spread.

Tunny fish salad

Tin of tunny fish
Lettuce
Watercress
Tomato or cucumber (if in season)
Hard-boiled egg (if available)
Salad dressing (given below)

Prepare lettuce and cress carefully and dry well. Line a salad bowl with crisp lettuce leaves, keeping some of the smaller ones for garnishing. Break or tear remainder of lettuce lightly, also the watercress. Put these in a bowl with the fish flaked. Mix very lightly with the dressing and put in centre of the salad bowl. Decorate neatly with remainder of lettuce, watercress and the other salad stuffs.

Salad dressing without oil

Mix together:-
2 teaspoonsful white flour
2 small teaspoonsful white sugar
1 ½ teaspoonsful dry mustard
Spoonful salt

Then stir in ½ pint water and beat until mixed. Beat one egg (or dried), 2 level teaspoonsful margarine or butter. Cook slowly over boiler until fat dissolves and mixture thickens, stirring constantly. Bottle when cold. Keeps for months.

N Mahy

Savoury Dishes

Minced cabbage

1 cabbage
Butter, fat or oil
1 oz flour
2 tablespoonsful vinegar
Salt and pepper
Hard boiled eggs

Boil and press the
cabbage quite dry
and chop finely. Heat
the butter or fat (if
oil, it must always be
left till a blue haze
comes from the pan).
Sprinkle in flour, mix
smoothly and put in
the cabbage. Add salt
and pepper to taste,
put in the vinegar,
stir over the fire for
5 or 6 minutes, then
serve garnished with
sections of hard-
boiled eggs. Nice with
mashed potatoes.

Savoury porridge

Boil one or two onions
or more as required;
when sufficiently cooked
thicken with oatmeal as
for porridge. Season with
pepper and salt or curry
powder.

Paté

1 lb sausage meat
1 tablespoonful rice
1 large carrot
1 small onion or two shallots or garlic (if preferred)
½ teacupful breadcrumbs, salt, pepper, parsley

Boil rice, which when boiled should fill a teacup,
grate carrot and onion, chop parsley. Mix all
ingredients together and bake in a moderate oven
for about one hour. If you have a small piece of
greaseproof paper, cover over when baking. When
cold this will make a fine sandwich spread.

Curried lentils

2 ozs lentils, soaked and cooked
1 oz butter
1 oz oatmeal flour
1 dessertspoon curry powder
1 small apple
1 onion or half a leek
Salt and pepper
Little stock from vegetables

Melt the butter and fry onion or leek (cut up) till
golden brown, add apple shredded (don't peel)
and cook till soft, then add the flour and curry
powder. Stir in the stock and cook till thickened,
simmer ½ hour and then add lentils, salt and
pepper.
Serves 4

Parsnip croquettes

4 large parsnips
1 egg
2 dessertspoonsful breadcrumbs
2 dessertspoonsful chopped parsley
1 oz butter or oil for frying

Peel and wash parsnips and cut in half. Put in boiling water with a little salt. Cook until tender. Take out and drain well. Brush them over with the egg well beaten, roll in the breadcrumbs. Fry in a little butter or oil until a nice brown. Sprinkle with chopped parsley. Potatoes can be used instead of parsnips, using about 1 lb mashed potatoes to same ingredients.

Hint: save all pieces of bread and when you have use of the oven, brown these, and make very fine bread crumbs; use these for frying. This saves fat and does not stick to the frying pan. Use half a teaspoon of fat only to fry potato cakes for 15 minutes. Cover with a large saucepan lid to keep the heat in.

Vegetable pie

1½ lbs mashed potatoes
1 large turnip
2 medium carrots
½ lb haricot beans or green peas
½ lb tomatoes
1 oz butter
¼ pint of gravy or brown sauce

Grease a pie dish and arrange the sliced turnip, carrots, tomatoes and peas or beans in layers. Pour over ¼ pint brown sauce or gravy. Cover with mashed potatoes and put butter on top broken into small pieces. Bake in a fairly hot oven about half an hour. Butter can be omitted; it is quite nice without.

Haricots

1 lb haricot beans
1 oz butter
2 tablespoons chopped parsley
Pepper and salt

Soak the beans overnight in cold water. Cook in boiling unsalted water until soft. Drain off the liquor (which should be saved as vegetable stock), reheat the beans with butter. Add the chopped parsley with salt and pepper. Shake well over the heat (serve hot).

Homemade paste

¼ lb beans or peas
¼ oz fat
1 Oxo

Boil beans till soft, then mix Oxo till dissolved and rub through sieve. Mix in fat and salt and pepper. If fish paste is preferred, omit Oxo and flavour with anchovy essence.

Mrs Le Quesne,
Pomona Road, St Helier

Mock fish cakes

Take a basinful of mashed potatoes and add a teaspoonful each of mixed herbs, egg powder and salt and pepper to taste; mix well with a teaspoonful of anchovy essence. Make into round flat cakes and fry in hot fat to a golden brown.

Poverty cakes

Scraps of meat or fish can be turned to good account and made to go a long way if mixed with the following ingredients: One egg, two cupsful of milk, quarter teaspoonful baking powder, pinch of salt and sufficient flour to make a paste. Roll out as for a scone, cut in squares or rounds and fry in hot fat. The cakes should puff up and are very light.

Pastry without Butter

1 lb flour
1 teaspoonful of baking powder
Small wineglassful of salad oil
Water

Mix the flour and baking powder. Add the oil to cold water and stir the paste to a proper consistency for rolling. Fold it over and roll it out two or three times. Bake immediately.

Leek pie

Line a large plate with the above paste, cut up some leeks very finely, put on paste, add pepper and salt, if possible a little fat or butter, cover with paste, bake to a golden brown about 20 to 30 minutes.

Mrs M Jouault, Vallée des Vaux

Pasta

Occasionally products appeared in the rations which baffled traditional cooks. Following a letter to the Evening Post from "perplexed" several recipes containing pasta were submitted by other readers.

Macaroni

½ cup of broken macaroni or vermicelli
1 onion
4 or 5 tomatoes sliced

Soak macaroni in a little warm water fry onion till brown; add sliced tomatoes. Fry together for a few minutes: add macaroni with the water, add salt and pepper to taste. Put mixture in dish and bake in oven for half an hour. If impossible to use oven, leave in frying pan and cook slowly for half an hour. The above recipe can be varied in the following way: ½ cup of cooked minced meat, onion and macaroni. Tomatoes optional.

Vermicelli & tomato

Boil 2 ozs vermicelli and strain. Cut up finely one shallot or small onion and 1lb peeled tomatoes and cook them together to a pulp. Season and pour over the vermicelli. Serve very hot.

Macaroni with cheese sauce

Boil 2 ozs macaroni in salted water till tender. Strain and keep the liquid. Thicken the latter with a tablespoonful of barley flour, and add a good slice of camembert cut up small, and if possible a little milk. Pour all over the macaroni and brown for a few minutes in the oven or under the grill.

Tomato sauce

1 ½ cups Oxo brown sauce
Tomato purée
Salt and pepper
1 tablespoon minced onion
1 teaspoon butter

Melt butter in a saucepan, stir in onion, cook slowly till soft. Add brown sauce, bring to boil and flavour to taste with tomato purée. Season to taste with salt and pepper if necessary.

Potato Dishes

Potato flour

Wash thoroughly a quantity of potatoes, mince in food mincer or grate on medium-size grater. Put this pulp in bowl or pan or zinc bath, and cover well with water. (This water will be brown and frothy). Allow to stand about one hour. Carefully pour off as much of the water as possible without disturbing the pulp. It is better to dip it off with a cup or ladle. Refill pan and let it stand another hour. Do this three or four times; the last water should be nearly clear. Then take the potato pulp carefully out, squeeze and drain it in colander or sieve into another pan. Let the water stand another hour or, better still, overnight. Now carefully remove all the water with cup or ladle, and the flour will be found in the bottom of the pan. Put this on shallow plates or dishes, and dry in a warm room or in the sun. (Not on any account in the oven, lest the flour becomes sour or jelly). This takes several days and must be stirred frequently. It is impossible to say how much flour you get to the cabot of potatoes, as some potatoes contain more than others. As the flour dries, it whitens.

Potato flaky pastry

1 cupful flour
2 tablespoonsful fat
½ teaspoonful salt
2 cupsful cold mashed potatoes
1 teaspoonful baking powder
Milk

Mash potatoes very smoothly. Mix with flour sifted with the baking powder and salt. Add milk (if necessary) to give a light dough, soft but dry. Roll out. Dab over one-third of the fat. Fold in three and again roll out. Repeat this process three times then use for covering pies.

Pommes-de-terre en sauce blanche

Take 3lbs potatoes, slice them, put in saucepan, cover with water; add a sprig of parsley, thyme and any piece of celery left over, a pinch of pepper and salt, and leave to cook till tender. Take 2 tablespoons of flour and smooth down to thin paste with a little milk. Pour into saucepan without straining the potatoes. If cream available ½ cup may be added just prior to serving. We have eaten the above many winters now and have always enjoyed it.

Mrs P

Potato cakes

12 ozs cooked potatoes
3 ozs flour, parsley, salt
1 oz butter (optional)

Mash potatoes finely with butter or a tablespoon of milk. Add finely chopped parsley. Work in flour and salt. Roll out thinly, cut into round cakes and cook on a flat baking tin for about ten minutes.

Mock suet pudding

8 ozs plain flour (more or less as required)
Salt and pepper to taste
2 good-sized raw peeled potatoes

Put the flour or seasoning in a mixing bowl. Grate the potato finely, and add to the flour, mixing with cold water until the right dough is obtained. Put in a greased basin and steam for at least two hours. This recipe is suitable as a plain pudding or as dumplings and also makes a good crust for any filling such as apples. I have also used it for vegetable pudding. Slightly cooking the vegetables first. For those who have it, the addition of baking powder or bicarbonate of soda is an added improvement.

Mrs Minnear,
St Ouen

Potato and tomato casserole

2 lbs potatoes
1 tin tomatoes
1 oz butter
Pepper and salt

Melt butter in a small pan and add potatoes cut into quarter-inch slices. Put potatoes in the fat for a few minutes over a low gas. Turn into pie-dish, cover with tomatoes and a little pepper and salt. Bake in a moderate oven until brown. The liquor from tomatoes may be used according to taste.

Tomato and potato pie

1 tin tomatoes
Potatoes according to need
Some mixed herbs
A little fat if possible
Pepper and salt to taste

Boil and mash potatoes with the fat and mixed herbs. Take some of the tomatoes and put in the bottom of a fairly deep dish, then some potatoes and more tomatoes, finishing with potatoes. Bake in a moderate oven until quite brown on top. Heat the juice of the tomatoes and use as a sauce or, if preferred, keep for soup. I have also made this dish with Swedes or carrots, leaving out the tomatoes, and mashing the other vegetables with the potatoes.

Baked pudding

4 tablespoons flour or
flour and oatmeal
1 ½ tablespoonsful fat (of
any kind)
1 ½ tablespoonsful sugar
2 ½ teacupsful mashed
potato
Pinch of nutmeg, spice or
grated lemon rind
1 teaspoonful baking
powder or egg powder
Milk (quantity depends
on kind of potatoes)

Rub fat into flour. Stir
in all dry ingredients
and gradually work in
the mashed potatoes.
Mix very well with
the milk (consistency
should be rather
stiff). Spread thinly
on greased baking
tin. Cook till a golden
brown. NB if allowed to
become nearly cold and
then cut into squares
or fingers, when cold
they can be served as
biscuits at teatime.

Use for potato peelings

Now that the new potatoes need peeling, it
is a pity to waste the peelings. Of course, if
you have rabbits, they will eat them either
cooked or raw, but if not, dry them and
use as fuel. They are fine for the copper or
boiler or to bank up a fire with a little ash
or cinders added.

Scalloped potatoes

2lbs potatoes
A little flour
½ pint milk
Pepper and salt
1 small onion or leek
Tablespoon of breadcrumbs

Peel potatoes and cut in quarter-inch slices.
Arrange in layers in a pie dish. Put a little flour,
finely chopped onion, pepper and salt between
each layer. Pour over the milk, sprinkle potatoes
with breadcrumbs and bake in a moderate oven
until golden brown. Served with limpet omelette,
scalloped potatoes are enjoyed more.

The seaweed known as carrageen,
or Irish moss, could be collected
by those allowed onto the seashore
and used to replace gelatine.

How to prepare carrageen moss

The moss must be placed in a pan of fresh water in the open and, if
possible, in the sunshine, as the more direct light the carrageen receives
the better it will bleach. Change the water twice daily and continue
until the smell of seaweed has almost disappeared. This will take
approximately seven days. Having done this, it should be dried in the
sunshine. When thoroughly dry it may be put into tins or jars where it will
keep indefinitely.

Invalid drinks

These can be made in two ways: one by adding ¼ of a pint of jelly when strained to ½ pint of boiling milk with a little sugar; this is very nourishing as a nightcap.

The second is made by adding 1oz of moss to two quarts of cold water and soaking overnight; bring to boil and simmer till reduced by half; strain and add sugar to taste and lemon juice. If it should be too thick when cold, add a little more water.

Milk jelly

¼ oz moss
1 pint cold water
¾ pint hot milk
Sugar and flavour to taste

Soak moss for one hour in the water, bring to boil and simmer for 20 minutes. Strain and press with wooden spoon to get all the jelly; add the hot milk, sugar and flavouring and mix well together and put into glasses. This will set in half an hour.

Blancmange

This is made in the same way as milk and jelly by adding 4 tablespoonsful of brown or white flour mixed in a little of the cold milk. Add to the remainder of the milk and the jelly and bring all to the boil.

Bramble jelly

2 lbs blackberries
½ oz carrageen moss (one teacup)
Saccharines to taste (approximately 10-12)
Or a little sugar

Heat and strain blackberries as for jelly. Soak moss in just sufficient water to cover for one hour, then simmer for about 20 minutes.
Add to the blackberry juice and cook gently together until moss is entirely dissolved. Remove from fire and stir in saccharines which have been dissolved in a very little water.

Galantine

1 pint of jelly made by adding ¾ oz moss to 1 pt of water to get a thick jelly
4 oz minced meat
3 tablespoonsful of flour or 1 pint of mixed vegetables cooked and mashed
a little onion, mixed herbs, pepper and salt

Mix all well together, put into a basin and steam for 1 ½ hours. When cold turn out and serve.

Puddings

Plain Jane

(adapted from E. Craig's recipe)

1 teacup plain flour or flour and oatmeal
1 ½ tablespoonsful fat (of any kind)
1 ½ tablespoonsful sugar
2 ½ cupsful grated raw potato
Pinch of spice (not necessary)
½ teaspoonful bicarbonate soda or
1 teaspoonful baking powder
Milk

Rub fat into flour. Mix all dry ingredients well. Stir in enough milk to make a rather soft consistency and beat thoroughly. Turn into a greased tin and bake till firm or turn into a greased pudding bowl and steam for 2 hours. If using a hay box, cook 30 minutes on a fire and 3 hours in hay box.

Hasty pudding

1 pint milk
1 dessertspoon sugar
1 tablespoon flour
1 oz margarine or little butter
Nutmeg

Mix the flour to a cream with a little cold milk, boil the rest of the milk and add the margarine and sugar, stir, then mix with the flour. Boil again for 2 minutes, stirring all the time. Pour into a buttered pie dish, put one or two small pieces of margarine on the surface, add some grated nutmeg and bake in a moderate oven for 10 minutes.

Plain flour blancmange

Mix the flour with a drop of cold milk. Boil the remainder with the sugar and butter. Be sure the mixture is quite smooth. Pour in gradually the boiled milk, stirring all the time, return to the pan and boil up until it thickens. Pour into a mould previously soaked in cold water and leave until set. If one has it, flavouring or colouring essence is an improvement.

Bread pudding

4 slices of bread
Apple purée (very little)
Spice (if you have any) or
Nutmeg
1 pint milk
1 egg
A few sultanas or currants

Spread apple purée on the bread and cut in slices. Place in the bottom of a pie dish. Add spice, or nutmeg, also sultanas or currants. Whisk egg with the milk and pour gently over mixture. Let it stand for one hour and bake for ½ hour in a moderate oven. Enough for three to four persons.

Cocoa steamed pudding

2 desertspoons of cocoa
1 oz butter
½ lb breadcrumbs
1 gill milk
2 dessertspoons sugar
½ teaspoon vanilla essence
1 tablespoon flour
1 egg

Mix all dry ingredients together and rub in the butter. Separate the egg yolk from the white and stir the beaten yolk in with the vanilla and milk. Whisk the white to a very stiff froth and fold in as lightly as possible. Place the mixture at once into a greased basin, cover with grease-proof paper and steam for 1 ½ hours. This is very good for children. For three persons.

Mrs Ann Kayens, Millbrook

One week, a ration of seven ounces of dates became available and Miss Fraser, the cookery expert, submitted the following:

Date pudding No. 1

½ teacup breadcrumbs
1 teacup breakfast meal or ½ teacup breakfast meal and ½ teacup flour
1 tablespoon of fat of any kind or 1 tablespoon oil
3 ozs stoned and chopped dates
½ tablespoonful sugar
Level tablespoonful bicarbonate of soda
Pinch of salt
Milk, or milk and water, to make stiff dough

Rub fat or oil into the flour. Mix all dry ingredients together. Add enough liquid to make a stiff dough. Turn into a greased bowl, cover with greased paper. Steam for about 1 –1 ¼ hrs. SAUCE: stew the date stones in a half-pint of milk or milk and water. Strain and thicken with dessertspoonful of breakfast meal or potato flour mixed to a cream with a little water. Boil up well, sweeten and flavour to taste, pour round the pudding.

Date pudding No: 2

1 teacup flour and breakfast meal, or breakfast meal only
1 teacup scraps of bread
1 ½ tablespoons fat or oil
¼ lb stoned dates
½ tablespoon sugar
Level teaspoonful bicarbonate of soda
Water

Soak bread in cold water. After soaking squeeze out all the water and beat the bread with a fork to take away any lumps. Add the flour and other dry ingredients. Stir in the oil or fat previously melted. Mix to rather a stiff batter with cold water. Turn into a greased baking-tin and bake till firm and brown, or if preferred steam for 1-1 ¼ hours. NB: if you like, a tablespoonful of cocoa substitute could be added.

"The barley flour ration which is being issued should prove to be an asset, particularly where there are children, hence the reason for its being granted to juveniles. It can be used in many ways and here are a few".

Miss Fraser

Baked Pudding

Mix the flour smoothly with cold milk and put remainder on the heat. Pour hot milk on to blended barley flour. Return to pan – bring to boil stirring well. Cook for about 10 mins, sweeten and flavour. Turn into greased pie dish – bake till lightly browned.

Steamed pudding

2 ozs barley flour
2 ozs potato flour or breakfast food
1 oz fat
1 tablespoon sugar
¼ teaspoon bicarbonate of soda
Milk, preferably butter milk or sour milk

Mix dry ingredients together. Rub in fat and make well in centre. Stir in enough milk to make soft dough and mix well. Turn into greased pudding bowl, cover with greased paper and steam for ¾ hour.
NB: Instead of steaming, this mixture could be baked.

Cakes & Biscuits

Baking powder

Mix well together:
4 ozs ground rice
4 ozs bicarbonate of soda
3 ozs tartaric acid.

Pass them through a sieve. Keep in an airtight tin.

Barley flour scones

½ lb barley flour
½ pint milk and water
¼ teaspoonful salt
Baking powder

Mix into light dough, and bake in very hot oven 15 to 20 minutes.

Barley flour biscuits

2 ozs barley flour
2 ozs potato flour or breakfast food
1 oz fat
1 oz sugar
Pinch of salt
¼ teaspoonful bicarbonate of soda
3 or 4 tablespoons milk (preferably butter milk or sour milk)
Spice (if liked)

Sieve barley flour and other flour. Rub in fat and add sugar, salt and bi-carb. Mix to a very stiff dough with the milk. Turn on to a board and knead lightly till free from cracks. Roll out to about 1/8 inch thick. Cut into biscuits and prick well with a fork. Place on lightly greased or floured baking tin. Bake in a quick oven till lightly browned (10-15 minutes).

Barley flour drop scones

½ lb barley flour
1 tablespoonful sugar or syrup
½ egg or 1 teaspoonful of egg powder
½ teaspoonful baking powder or bicarbonate of soda
¼ teaspoonful salt
½ pint buttermilk or milk and water

Mix all dry ingredients, beat egg well and add milk to it and mix to a batter. Grease hot frying pan with any fat or cooking oil. Drop spoonful into pan (about three or four can be cooked at once to save fat). When brown on one side, turn and brown on the other. Wrap in a clean towel.

Biscuits

1 ½ tablespoonsful cocoa substitute
3 tablespoonsful barley flour or
breakfast meal
3 tablespoonsful semolina
1 ½ tablespoonsful fat or
2 tablespoonsful oil
1 tablespoonful sugar
¼ teaspoonsful bicarbonate of soda
Milk to bind

Rub fat into flour and mix all dry
ingredients. Mix to a stiff dough
with milk. Turn on to a floured
board and knead till free from
cracks. Roll out to ¼ inch thick.
Stamp into rounds and prick with
a fork to prevent rising. Put on a
greased tray and bake for about 15-
20 minutes (allow to cool on a tray
before lifting off).

Rock buns with brown flour

½ lb brown flour
Pinch salt
1 teaspoonful baking powder
1 ½ ozs butter
3 ozs sugar (brown if possible)
1 egg
A little milk
A little nutmeg

Sift the flour, salt and baking
powder, then rub in the butter, add
the sugar and nutmeg. Beat the egg
with a little milk and mix the whole
into a stiff paste. Put on a greased
baking-tin in rough shapes. Bake for
20 minutes. Mark 6.

How to use brown flour

"Many people seem to find
difficulty in using the brown flour
which is now part of the usual
weekly ration. Several have been
heard to complain that apart
from using it instead of porridge
they can do little with it. Here is a
recipe for small cakes taken from
a vegetarian cookery book which
has been tried and tested in the
home of one of the E.P. reporters
and found to be excellent"

Small cakes

4 oz flour
2 tablespoonsful butter
2 tablespoonsful sugar
1 teaspoonful of cinnamon or mixed
spice
1 egg or 1 teaspoonful of egg powder
½ teaspoonful bicarbonate of soda

Cream sugar and butter, add
beaten egg, mix in flour, then add
soda dissolved in milk. Lastly add
cinnamon or mixed spice. Place in
patty tins and bake in a hot oven for
15 minutes.

Buns

6 tablespoons white flour
6 tablespoons brown flour
7 tablespoons sugar
Pinch salt
1 ½ teaspoonsful baking powder
Pinch bicarbonate of soda
3 or 4 teaspoons vinegar
8 dried prunes, cut up small
(or dry fruit)
Milk to mix

Mix all the ingredients and bake for
½ to ¾ hour in hot oven.

Family scones

8 ozs white flour
8 ozs brown flour
6 ozs sugar
3 ozs fat
4 ozs fruit or nuts
½ teaspoonful baking powder
½ teaspoonful bicarbonate of soda
A pinch of salt
¼ pint milk and water or skimmed milk

Sift flour. Add all dry ingredients.
First rub in fat. Mix to a stiff paste.
Bake in a hot oven for 20 minutes.

Mrs A Brasford, St Mary

Biscuits made with brown flour

9 ozs oat flour
2 ozs butter
1 ½ ozs moist sugar
Small teaspoon ground ginger
Small teaspoon baking powder or egg
substitute
¼ gill half milk half water
Pinch salt

Sift the flour, add the dry
ingredients, melt the butter and
then mix all together. Make into
thin biscuits with a cutter or small
cup. Bake for 20 minutes, till brown,
in a moderate oven.

Staffordshire oat-cakes

½ lb oat flour
1 level teaspoonful cream of tartar
½ level teaspoonful bicarbonate of soda
½ pint milk
Pinch salt

Sift flour, tartar and salt together,
dissolve soda in milk and mix to a
batter, not so thin as for pancakes.
Grease a hot frying-pan (a cast-iron
pan or griddlestone is best). Pour
in ½ cupful, the size of a saucer and
turn when brown. Usually toasted
and buttered, or eaten with cheese.

Date rock-buns

1 teacupful bran (sieved from breakfast meal or flour)
4 ozs chopped dates
level teaspoon bicarbonate of soda
½ tablespoon fat of any kind, or cooking oil
½ tablespoon sugar
Milk to bind

Heat oven and grease baking-tin. Mix all dry ingredients, but keep back a few pieces of the chopped dates to put on the top of the buns. Make a well and stir in the oil or melted fat. Add enough milk to make a dough. Place the mixture in rough heaps on the greased tin and put a piece of chopped date on top of each. Bake in a quick oven till browned (Regulo 6). NB: if preferred, the mixture can be made softer, then spread into a sandwich-tin, baked till brown and then cut into sections.

Scones without fat

10 oz white flour
6 oz oat flour
1 tablespoon sugar or 1 tablespoon syrup
1 teaspoon baking powder
1 teaspoon bicarbonate of soda
Buttermilk to mix

Sieve flour, bicarbonate of soda and baking powder, add sugar (or if syrup used, mix in cup of buttermilk and add). Add enough buttermilk to make a dough, knead lightly and roll out quarter-inch thick, cut into rounds and bake for 15 minutes. Regulo 5.

Mrs Romeril

Scones

Sift ½ lb oat flour, 1 level teaspoonful cream of tartar, ½ level teaspoonful baking powder and ½ level teaspoonful bicarbonate of soda together. Rub 1 oz butter into the flour, add 1 teaspoonful castor sugar and mix to a paste with a quarter pint of milk. Roll out to fit a 9 inch sandwich pan. Mark in sections and bake for 20 minutes in a moderately heated oven. When cooked, cut into sections, split open and butter or serve with syrup.

Cake

7 tablespoonsful flour
3 tablespoonsful sugar
Pinch salt
1 teaspoon egg powder or custard
1 teaspoon baking powder
2 teaspoons vinegar
Pinch bicarbonate soda
Milk to mix
Fruit to taste

Bake 1 hour in gas oven.

Pudding or cake mixture

1 teacupful flour of any kind
1 teacupful breakfast meal or semolina
2 tablespoonsful fat
2 or 3 tablespoonsful of sugar
2 or 3 tablespoonsful cocoa substitute
Milk
½ teaspoonful bicarbonate of soda dissolved in a tablespoonful vinegar

Mix all dry ingredients except bicarbonate of soda. Rub in the fat and mix to rather a soft consistency with the milk (cannot give exact quantity, because it depends on the kind of flour used). Dissolve bicarbonate in vinegar and add to the mixture. Beat thoroughly. Turn into a greased pudding bowl and cover. Steam for 1 ½ hours. Or turn into prepared cake tin and bake until risen and browned for 1 ¼ hours.

Milk biscuits

½ lb flour
Pinch of salt
1 teaspoonful baking powder
1 oz fat
1 gill milk

Mix dry ingredients together, then melt fat and add the milk, making it just warm. Pour into the centre of the flour and mix all together to a fairly stiff dough. Knead on floured board until free from cracks. Roll out thinly, cut out circles with a cutter and prick out with a fork. Place on a tin, bake in moderate oven, taking care the oven is not too hot.

Oatmeal biscuits

3 ozs flour
3 ozs oatmeal flour
¼ teaspoon salt
1 oz butter
1 ½ ozs sugar
½ teaspoon baking powder

Mix all dry ingredients, rub in butter, add milk to a very stiff dough. Turn onto a floured board and roll out thinly, cut with a cutter, place on a greased tin and prick with a fork. Bake in a moderate oven for 15 minutes.

Ginger cake No.1

6 ozs wheat flour
4 ozs fine breadcrumbs (crusts included)
1 dessertspoonful ground ginger
2 dessertspoonsful sugar
1 teaspoonful baking powder
Pinch bicarbonate of soda
Fruit may be added if you have it
½ pint milk to mix

May be eaten hot as bread pudding or cold

Ginger cake No.2

½ lb oatmeal flour
¼ lb white flour
1 teaspoon ginger
1 tablespoonful syrup or 2ozs sugar
1 tablespoonful glycerine or any fat
1 teaspoon bicarbonate of soda
3 teaspoons vinegar
¼ pint milk

Well mix together oatmeal flour, white flour and ginger. Beat up glycerine with syrup and a little milk; if sugar and fat is used, mix with flour. Mix beaten up glycerine with flour, etc. Then add bicarbonate of soda to remainder of milk in a large cup, add vinegar, and while all this is bubbling, add to mixture. Bake ½ to ¾ hour in a moderate oven Regulo 4 or 5.

Small chocolate cakes

2 ozs bran breakfast food
1 oz infant's food
1 oz wheat flour
1 dessertspoonful cocoa
1 heaped dessertspoonful sugar
Pinch bicarbonate of soda
1 teaspoonful baking powder
1 teaspoonful caraway seeds if liked
Milk (or milk and water) to mix

Put a spoonful in each of 12 'shell' tins. Makes 12 little cakes. Bake 20 to 30 minutes.

C W

Chinese cake

¼ lb brown sugar
2 ozs butter or fat
½ teaspoonful salt
½ teaspoonful cinnamon
1 teaspoonful ground cloves
¼ pint hot water
½ lb brown flour
½ teaspoonful bicarbonate of soda

Beat together the fat and sugar. Add the salt, cloves and some of the hot water. Beat well, then add the remainder of the water, the flour and the soda dissolved in 1 teaspoonful of hot water. Mix well, pour into greased tin and bake for 1 ¼ hours Regulo mark 4. The cake improves with keeping.

Luncheon cake

½ lb white flour
¼ lb oatmeal flour
2 ozs fat (if dripping is
used and a few drops of
lemon juice)
1 teaspoon baking
powder
1 teaspoon egg powder or
2 teaspoons baking
powder if no egg powder
available
Milk or skim milk to mix
4 ozs fruit or flavouring
such as almond, etc.
3 or 4 ozs sugar

Rub fat into flour,
oatmeal and baking
powder which have
been well mixed,
preferably sieved. Add
sugar and fruit, mix
to a moderately soft
mixture.

Bake in a fairly hot
oven for about 1 hour
Regulo 5.

Caraway seed cake
(Large family size)

6 ozs flour
4 ozs oatmeal flour
1 ½ tablespoons caraway seed
1 ½ tablespoons sugar
1 tablespoon butter
1 egg
Pinch salt
1 ½ teaspoons baking powder or
Andrews salts
¼ teaspoon cream of tartar
Milk

Mix all dry ingredients and rub in butter till like
fine crumbs. Whisk egg in milk, beat all together
with a wooden spoon. Put in a well greased cake
tin and bake for 1 ½ hours in a moderate oven
(Regulo 5). When three-quarters cooked reduce
oven Regulo 3. (Don't have mixture too dry).
Before taking cake out test with a skewer; if it
comes out clean, cake is done. The rind and juice
of one lemon could be used instead of the caraway
seed, or one good tablespoon of cocoa.

Preserves

At one time the Evening Post carried several recipes for carrot jam. They all use lemons, so maybe some had arrived in the island.

Carrot jam

Mrs J H Valpy, of Grouville Rectory, writes: "I used the following recipe during the last war and also lately, and can recommend it."

To each pound of carrot pulp allow one pound of sugar
2 lemons
2 tablespoonsful brandy
6 bitter almonds

Wash and scrape carrots, cut up and put into pan with boiling water to cover. Cook until tender, then rub through sieve and weigh pulp. Put in pan with sugar in above proportion. Let sugar dissolve, then boil fast until a thick paste, probably quarter of an hour, keep stirring all the time to prevent burning. When mixture has cooled slightly, add grated rind and strained juice of lemons, also brandy and almonds, having shelled and halved them.

Mrs C Vilton, 34 St Mark's Road states:-

Slice 4 lbs carrots into thin pieces, barely cover them with water. Simmer them steadily until quite soft. Now beat to a pulp with a wooden fork. Add 4 lbs sugar. Again bring slowly to the boil. Keep stirring for 5 minutes. When partly cooled stir in a few chopped bitter almonds, the finely-grated rind and the strained juice of a lemon, and two teaspoonsful of brandy. This last ensures the jam will keep. Ginger may also be added for flavouring.

Mrs Romeril, 64 Oxford Road, gives the following:-

3 lemons
1 lb carrots
3 lbs sugar
3 pints water

Scrape carrots, cut lemons small as for marmalade, add the water, soak for 24 hours. Boil 1 hour, then add sugar and boil 1 hour or longer until it sets.

Mrs Kayne's recipe is:-

2 carrots (large size)
1 tablespoon sugar
Juice of ½ a lemon
½ oz gelatine

This makes one pound. Peel carrots. Wash well. Grate very fine, put in a saucepan with sugar and add very little water. To prevent burning stir until tender, put through a sieve, with strained lemon juice. Dissolve gelatine in ¼ gill hot water and add to mixture.

Mrs S Leschery, Bellozanne Avenue sends us a recipe using less sugar:

2 lbs carrots grated or minced finely, put under water and left to soak for 48 hours
2 tins grapefruit instead of lemons
About 1 ½ ozs gelatine crystals or 4 or 5 sheets gelatine
1 ½ lbs sugar

Cut up grapefruit and add to carrots. Boil until carrots are soft then add grapefruit juice, sugar and gelatine. Boil another ½ hour.

Carrot and beetroot jam

Equal weights of carrots and beetroots
Sugar
Lemons

Weigh the carrots and beetroots, scrape the carrots, and boil them separately until tender. Pass through a coarse sieve, measure the purée, and to each pint allow 12 ozs of sugar and the juice of two lemons. Place the whole in a preserving pan, boil gently for ½ an hour, and turn the preparation into pots. If intended to be kept for some time, a glass of brandy should be added to each pint of jam before putting it into the pot. Keep closely covered in a dry, cool place.

Other carrot jam recipes are:

1 ½ breakfast cups of grated carrot
1 lb sugar
1 lemon

For this, use 1 ½ cups grated carrot or aim at producing the same quantity by boiling some carrots and, when tender, mashing them. Put the carrot in a pan, add sugar with the juice and grated rind of a lemon and stir while the sugar is melting. Then boil until the jam begins to set. At this point throw in a handful of blanched almonds cut into pieces. This may be used as an economical foundation for more expensive jams.

6 carrots
6 lemons
6 pints water
6 lbs sugar

Grate carrots, shred peel of four lemons, and add juice and pulp of all six. Put into water, boil for 1 ½ hours, then add sugar and boil for a further hour.

5 lbs sugar
6 lemons
3 lbs carrots
5 pints water

Peel and cut up lemons and soak for 48 hours in one pint of water. Wash, peel and grate carrots and boil them in the remaining four pints of water for half an hour, mix all together after lemons have soaked for 48 hours, add the 5 lbs of sugar and boil for an hour, stirring all the time.

Carrot marmalade No.1

2 lbs grated carrots
1 lb sugar
½ bottle lemon crystals

Grate the carrots, cover with water, and leave to stand overnight. Boil for ¾ hour, then add sugar and lemon crystals and boil for further ½ hour. If available, now add one gelatine leaf (previously dissolved in hot water), as the jam is removed from the heat. Tried and found to be jolly good.

Carrot marmalade No.2

4 large carrots
3 lbs sugar
4 lemons
4 pints water

Scrape carrots and lemons and squeeze juice, add the water and boil for 1 ½ hours then add sugar and boil for another hour.

Elderberry jelly

One quart of elderberries and one pint of water. Boil together for a few minutes, then press through a towel till all the juice is extracted. Take one quart of apples and one pint of water, boil together and extract the juice in the same way (the apples should be quartered before boiling). Now mix both juices together and to one pint of juice, take one pound of sugar and boil till it jellies nicely. The elderberry juice will not firm alone, but with apple juice it gives a beautiful jelly.

"B"

Homemade black butter

2 lb sweet apples
2 lbs sour apples
1 lemon
½ lb sugar
½ pint sweet cider
Spices and liquor if available
(I used 2 teaspoons mixed spice and 2
teaspoons cinnamon)

Peel and cut up apples and chop
lemon up small. Place apples and
lemon in cider and stew till pulp,
over a very low heat to prevent
burning. Then place in large bowl
or crock, add sugar and spices and
bake on a lower shelf in the oven
for two hours or more while dinner
is cooking. Stir often to prevent
burning or skin forming while in
oven. This makes about 1 ½ lbs of
black butter.

Potato jelly

First steam some peeled potatoes
until they will mash easily. Make a
syrup of sugar by adding water to it
and stirring over a slow fire. When
sugar is thoroughly dissolved, add
the mashed potatoes. There must
be no lumps. Boil sharply for 10
minutes. Add the juice of lemon or
ginger syrup for flavouring.

Mrs C Vilton, St Marks Road

'Answer to a Red Cross letter'

(Anonymous, abridged)

We are quite well, but getting thinner,
Not much for tea, less still for dinner,
Tho' not exactly on our uppers
We've said adieu to cold ham suppers.

In peacetime those who wished slim
Tried diet, massage, baths and Gym,
We'll tell the stout of every nation
The secret's solved by "Occupation."

Indeed it's getting quite the fashion
To queue up for our weekly ration,
Butter, sugar, tea and flour,
Salt, we wait for by the hour.

Men miss their beer, we have no hops
Children have no Lollipops,
What put most people in a hole
Was when they had to ration coal.

All are aware before the Battle,
Famous we were for Jersey Cattle,
When all is over, we're in the news
Famous for our Jersey stews.

Little Jersey bombed and mined,
To us War fates have proved unkind,
But after all the stress and strain,
To Greater Heights we'll rise again.'

Anonymous poem in the Jersey War Tunnels Collection, 2002/470

Bibliography

- Bird, M. 'News from the Kitchen Front' in 'Channel Islands Occupation Review 1974' (CIOS)
- Bird, M. 'News from the Kitchen Front' in 'Channel Islands Occupation Review 1975' (CIOS)
- Carr, G. 'Occupied Behind Barbed Wire' (Jersey Heritage, 2009)
- Cruickshank, C. 'The German Occupation of the Channel Islands' (Sutton, 2004)
- Ellison, G et al 'How did the Occupation Affect the Health of Channel Islanders' in 'Channel Islands Occupation Review No. 28' (CIOS, Guernsey, 2000)
- Garnier, V. 'Medical History of the Jersey Hospitals and Nursing Homes during the Occupation 1940-45' (Channel Islands Occupation Birth Cohort Study, 2002)
- Halliwell, M. 'Operating Under Occupation' (CIOS Jersey, 2005)
- Hillsdon, S. 'Jersey, Occupation Remembered' (Jarrold, 1986), McKinstry, Dr. N. & Darling, Dr. A. 'Survey of the Effects of the Occupation on the Health of the People of Jersey' (States of Jersey, 1945)
- Money, J. 'Aspects of War' (Channel Islands Publishing, 2011)
- Sanders, P. 'The British Channel Islands under German Occupation 1940-1945' (Jersey Heritage, 2005)
- Sinel, L. 'The German Occupation of Jersey' (Villette Publishing Limited, 1995)
- Turner, B. 'Outpost of Occupation' (Aurum, 2010), p127.
- Shirley Barr interviewed by Chris Addy, Jersey War Tunnels Collection
- Alan Nicolle interviewed by Chris Addy 27.07.2007, Jersey War Tunnels Collection record number 2009/67
- Conversation between Joseph Arthur Mière and the author, 2004